I love to hear the word MUFFINS. Thoughts of warm wonderful creations bursting with flavour and personality leap to mind. Memories of the last batch we baked or the one before urges me to try another! The possibility of creating a new and memorable combination of flavours or making the family favourite still fills me with excitement. Just quietly, there is another good part—the best part—we get to eat them. Nothing matches muffins with coffee or tea, for breakfast, morning tea, or just snacktime. Children and famished teenagers love them and find them a great mate for their after school binge. The savoury muffins are perfect with soup or as a dinner roll. Muffins make a healthy contribution to our diet.  Not too sweet, they are a vehicle for wonderfully nutritious ingredients, such as fruits, nuts, milk, eggs, yoghurt and lots of fibre. Most muffin recipes can easily be made free of cholesterol. They are so simple to make and best of all allow the cook great liberties. Almost any flavour combinations are possible with the minimum adjustment and for the impatient cook like me or the busy cook, their fast preparation and cooking time makes them a happy and useful addition to your cooking repertoire. Children will love to make these and you will enjoy letting them join you, mixing, watching them cook and then eating them. It is all a part of what I think is *Muffin Magic.*

Diana Linfoot
Home Economist Dip. HSc.

CONTENTS

HOW TO MAKE MAGIC MUFFINS
"Step by step"

1. Select your recipe
Sometimes it is hard to choose one recipe but some unloved bananas in the fruitbowl may be winking at you or some new seasons blueberries from the store may help your choice.

2. Prepare the muffin pans
It is essential to thoroughly grease the pans with either margarine or cooking spray. The pans can be lined with paper cases which give a softer edge to the muffins.

3. Preheat the oven
Because most muffins require a hot oven, it is adviseable to preheat the oven so it is responsive enough to cook the muffins quickly.

4. Assemble the ingredients
For best results, two bowls are required to make muffins. One is used for the wet mix and one to combine the dry ingredients before they are added to the wet mix. Standard measuring cups should be used for all recipes in the book.

5. Combine the Ingredients
Combine the wet and dry ingredients with a minimum of mixing. It is easy to overmix these ingredients. The mixture looks different for each recipe but should never become elastic. The desired mixture may look lumpy but as long as the dry ingredients are incorporated then the mixing is completed. Overmixed muffins are misshapen tough and dry, instead of moist and even textured with no tunnels.

6. Place the Mixture in Pans
A large spoon is good to transfer the batter to the pans. The mixture should be eased or carefully dropped into the pans and left as it falls. Do not flatten the tops. Any toppings are added now. Chopped nuts, sugar and spice, pieces of fruit add interest and appeal to muffins.

7. Bake the muffins
The recipe will indicate the recommended temperature. Usually 200°C is required but each oven varies and you may need to adapt the baking to your oven's personality. Usually

the middle rack of the oven is best. Your muffins are ready if they spring back when you touch them or when a cake tester or tooth pick comes out clean.

8. Removing muffins from the pan
Leave the muffins to "recover" when removed from the oven for 5 - 10 minutes before removing them from their pans, to cool. I like to "tuck them up" in a teatowel or cloth but if you like them crisp and crunchy on the edges place them on a wire rack to complete cooling.

9. Eating Muffins
Muffins can be eaten with or without butter. There are some delicious flavoured butters which can be simply made which add interest to your "Muffin Magic". Recipes are included in this book.

10. Storing Muffins
Most muffins will tolerate freezing. They need to be packed firmly, on a tray or in a container.

Cholesterol Free Muffins

Most recipes in this book can easily be made cholesterol free.
1. Omit the egg yolks using whites only.
2. Substitute full milk with skim milk.
3. Substitute yoghurt with fat free yoghurt.
4. Use vegetable oil in place of butter.

High fibre recipes make better cholesterol free muffins.

Apple Muffins

Ingredients

Wet Mix   2 cups grated raw apples
½ cup brown sugar
½ cup oil
2 eggs
1 teaspoon vanilla

Dry Mix   1 cup wholemeal self-raising flour
1 cup self-raising flour
¼ teaspoon baking soda
2 teaspoons cinnamon

Method:

Preheat the oven and grease the muffin pans. Thoroughly combine the wet mix ingredients. Combine the dry mix ingredients and mix thoroughly into the wet mix. Place the mixture in the prepared pans and bake.

Makes 12

Bake: at 200°C for 20-25 minutes.

Variations

Apple Raisin & Nut: Add ½ cup of chopped raisins, ½ cup of chopped walnuts and 1 tablespoon of grated lemon or orange rind to the wet mix.

Apple & Date: Add ¾ cup of finely chopped dates and 1 tablespoon grated lemon rind to the wet mix.

Apple & Ginger: Add ¼ cup of chopped crystallized ginger and 1 tablespoon of treacle to the wet mix. Add 1 teaspoon powdered ginger to the dry mix.

Apple & Bran: Substitute the wholemeal and self-raising flour with 1 cup of flaky bran and 1½ cups of self-raising flour.

Suggestion:
Sprinkle the top of the muffins with a mixture of equal parts of brown sugar and spice.

Comment:
These are lovely moist muffins and hardly need to be buttered. They will keep well, but are best kept refrigerated and then warmed before eating.

Apple & Raisin Muffins.

Apple Raisin & Allbran

Ingredients

Wet Mix   *1½ cups milk*
1½ cups allbran
2 eggs
1½ cups grated raw apple
½ cup raisins, chopped

Dry Mix   *¼ cup brown sugar*
½ teaspoons mixed spice
1½ cups self-raising flour

Method:

Preheat the oven and grease the muffin pans. Soak the allbran in the milk for 10-15 minutes until soft. Beat in the eggs and add the apple and raisins. Mix to combine. Mix the dry ingredients and then gently but thoroughly combine the wet mix with the dry mix. Place the mixture in the prepared tins. If necessary add a little extra liquid, or flour, to achieve the correct consistency. It should be possible to transfer the mixture to the pans on a spoon in one movement.

Makes 12

Bake: 200⁰C for 20-25 minutes.

Variations

Apple & Walnut Allbran: Substitute the raisins with ½ to 1 cup of walnuts.
Apple & Sultana Allbran: Substitute the raisins with ½ cup of sultanas.
Apple, Ginger and Walnut Allbran: Substitute the raisins with ½ cup of chopped walnuts and ¼ cup of chopped crystallized ginger.

Comment:

The allbran in these muffins gives them a lovely nutty flavour. They will keep well in a sealed container.

Apricot

Ingredients

Wet Mix   ½ cup margarine
½ cup sugar
2 eggs
1 cup yoghurt or milk
grated rind and juice of 1 orange
1 cup chopped dried apricots

Dry Mix   1½ cups self-raising flour

Method:
Preheat the oven and grease the muffin pans. Thoroughly blend the margarine and sugar and then beat in the remaining wet mix ingredients. Fold in the flour then place the mixture in the prepared pans and bake.

Makes 10-12

Bake: 200⁰C for 25 minutes.

Variations

Apricot & Almond: Add ½ cup of toasted slivered or chopped blanched almonds to the wet mix.

Apricot & Coconut: Add ½ cup dessicated coconut to the dry mix and ¼ cup additional orange juice to the wet mix.

Avocado Muffins.

Avocado

Ingredients

Wet Mix ¼ cup margarine
¼ cup sugar
1 egg
1 avocado, pureed
1 cup toasted slivered almonds
1 cup milk

Dry Mix 2 cups self-raising flour

Method:
Preheat the oven and grease the muffin pans. Cream the butter and sugar and beat in the egg. Blend in the avocado and milk and mix in the nuts. Lastly add the flour and mix gently but thoroughly, until the ingredients are moistened and combined. Place the mixture in the muffin pans and sprinkle the top of the muffins with equal parts of cinnamon and sugar before cooking.

Makes 12

Bake: 200⁰C for 20-25 minutes.

Comment:
These muffins have a delicate moist and nutty flavour. Serve with butter, honey butter or strawberry jam.

Banana

Ingredients

Wet Mix ½ cup butter 125g.
 ¼ cup sugar 63g
 1 egg
 1½ cups mashed bananas (about three medium bananas).

Dry Mix 1¾ cups self-raising flour 272g.
 ½ teaspoon nutmeg
 ¼ teaspoon baking soda

Method:

Preheat the oven and grease the muffin pans. Blend together the butter and sugar and then mix in the egg and banana. Combine the dry ingredients and then mix these into the wet ingredients. Place in the muffin tins and bake.

Makes 12-14

Bake: 200°C for 20-25 minutes

Variations

Banana & Chocolate Chip: Add ½ cup of chopped chocolate to the wet mix. ½ cup of chopped walnuts or pecans may be added as well.

Banana & Honey: Puree 1 large orange and add this with an extra egg to the wet mix. Increase the flour to 2 cups. Substitute the sugar with honey.

Banana and Mixed Fruit: Add 1½ cups of any desired combination of nuts and dried fruits to the wet mix. Chopped dried apricots, dates, pears, figs or sultanas, prunes or raisins are nice with the banana flavour.

Banana & Ginger: Add ½ cup of chopped glace ginger and ½ cup of chopped walnuts to the wet mix. Add 1½ teaspoons of cinnamon to the dry mix.

Banana & Bran

Ingredients

Wet Mix
½ cup margarine or oil
¼ cup sugar
2 eggs
¼ cup golden syrup
1½ cups mashed banana
1 tablespoon orange rind
½ cup milk or yoghurt

Dry Mix
1 cup flaky bran
2 cups self-raising flour
¼ teaspoon baking soda
½ teaspoon nutmeg

Method:
Preheat the oven and grease the muffin pans. Beat well, all of the wet mix ingredients and gently fold in the previously combined dry ingredients. Place in the muffin pans, sprinkle with topping and bake.

Makes 12-14

Bake: 200°C for 20-25 minutes.

Variations

Dried Fruit Banana Bran: ½ cup mixed dried fruits and nuts may be added to the wet mix as desired.

Topping: Cinnamon sugar (equal parts of cinnamon and sugar.)

Bran Muffins

Ingredients

Wet Mix ¼ cup butter, margarine or oil
¼ cup golden syrup
¼ cup sugar
2 eggs
1 cup milk

Dry Mix 1½ cups flaky bran
1 cup self-raising flour
1½ teaspoons mixed spice

Method:

Preheat the oven and grease the muffin pans.
Melt together the margarine and golden syrup.
Beat in the eggs, sugar and milk. Combine the
dry mix ingredients and fold into the wet mix.
Place in muffin pans and bake.

Makes 10

Bake: 150⁰C for 20-25 minutes.

Variations

Apple Bran: Add 1 cup of grated apple to the wet mix
and add 1 teaspoon of cinnamon or mixed spice and an
extra ¼ cup of flour to the dry mix.

Banana Bran: Substitute banana for the apple in the
Apple Bran mixture. Nuts may be added.

Blueberry Bran: Take a 450g tin of drained blue
berries and very gently fold these into the combined
mixture, taking care not to break the fruit.

Fresh Fruit Bran: Omit the milk from the wet mix and
add 1 cup pureed fresh fruit. This is a marvellous way
to utilise saggy, sad fruit from the fruit bowl.
Rockmelon, apples, oranges, watermelon, pears,
mangoes or a combination can be used.

Dried fruits and nuts added to this make the muffins
even more exciting. Jam can be used to substitute the
syrup and sugar. Substitute the sugar and syrup with
1 cup of jam.

Honey gives a good flavour with bran. Substitute the
sugar and syrup with ½ cup of honey.

Comment:

These muffins are very high in fibre.

Blueberry Muffins .

Blueberry

Ingredients

Wet Mix
½ cup butter
½ cup sugar
2 eggs
1 cup milk
¼ cup lemon juice
1 450 g tin blueberries, drained

Dry Mix 2½ cups self-raising flour

Method:
Preheat the oven and grease the muffin pans. Thoroughly blend the butter and sugar. Beat in the eggs and then the milk. Gently fold the drained blueberries into the mixture taking care not to break them. Fold the flour into the wet mix then place the mixture into the previously prepared pans and bake.

Makes 12

Bake: 200°C for 20-25 minutes.

Variations

Blueberry & Apple: Reduce the milk to ¼ cup and add 1 cup diced cooked or 1 cup grated raw apple. The cooking time will increase to 25-30 minutes.

Blueberry & Bran: Add 2 tablespoons of honey and an additional ½ cup of milk to the wet mix. Reduce the self-raising flour to 2 cups and add 1 cup of flaky bran to the dry mix.

Blueberry & Oatbran: See Oatbran muffins.

Carrot Muffins

Carrot Muffins

Ingredients

Wet Mix
- 3 eggs
- ½ cup sugar
- ½ cup oil
- 1 cup plain yoghurt
- 1 cup grated carrot
- ½ cup chopped walnuts

Dry Mix
- 3 cups self-raising flour
- ½ teaspoon baking soda
- 1 teaspoon cinnamon

Method:

Preheat the oven and grease the muffin pan. Beat together the eggs, sugar, oil and yoghurt. Add the carrot and walnuts. Fold in the previously combined dry mix. Place in muffin pans and bake.

Makes 12

Bake: 200⁰C for 20-25 minutes.

Variations

Carrot & Honey: Omit the sugar and add ½ cup honey to the wet mix. Increase the cinnamon to 2 teaspoons in the dry mix.

Carrot & Pineapple: Omit the yoghurt from the wet mix and add 1 cup crushed of pineapple. ½ cup currants may be added to the wet mix if desired.

Carrot & Sesame: Replace the walnuts with ½ to ¾ cup toasted sesame seeds and ½ cup sultanas.

Zucchini: Substitute grated raw zucchini for grated carrot in any of the above recipes. Add 1 tsp of vanilla essence to the wet mix.

Chocolate Chip

Ingredients

Wet Mix ½ cup butter or margarine
½ cup sugar
2 eggs
1 cup milk
½ cup yoghurt
1 teaspoon vanilla
½ cup chopped chocolate or chocolate chips

Dry Mix 3 cups self-raising flour

Method:

Preheat the oven and grease the muffin pans. Thoroughly blend the margarine and sugar and beat in the eggs, milk, yoghurt and vanilla. Mix in the chocolate chips. Gently fold the flour into the combined wet mix. Place in prepared pans and bake.

Makes 12-14

Bake: 180ºC for 15-20 minutes.

Variations

Double Choc: Add 2 tablespoons of cocoa blended with 4 tablespoons of boiling water to the combined wet mix.

Choc & Raisin &/or Pecan: Add ½ cup chopped raisins and or ½ cup chopped pecans to the combined wet mix of Choc or Double Choc muffins.

Chocolate Macaroon: Add ½ cup dessicated coconut to any of the above chocolate recipes.

Chocolate Chip Peanut Butter: See Peanut Butter Muffins.

Chocolate Chip & Banana: See Banana Muffins.

Coconut Muffins

Coconut

Ingredients

Wet Mix   ¼ cup butter or margarine
                ½ cup sugar
                2 eggs
                1½ cups milk
                or
                1½ cups plain yoghurt

Dry Mix   2½ cups self-raising flour
                1 cup macaroon dessicated
                coconut

Method:

Preheat the oven and grease the muffin pan. Thoroughly blend the butter and sugar then beat in the eggs and milk or yoghurt. Gently fold the combined dry mix into the wet mix. Place in prepared tins and top with the previously combined sugar and coconut topping. Bake the muffins.

Makes 12 medium muffins

Bake: 180⁰C for 25 minutes.

Variations

Coconut & Orange: Reduce the milk or yoghurt to ½ cup. Add ½ of cup blended, or pureed whole orange to the wet mixture, or ½ of cup orange juice and 2 tablespoons of grated orange rind to the wet mixture.

Coconut & Apricot: See Apricot Muffins.

Coconut & Cherry: Add 1 cup of chopped glace cherries to the combined wet mix.

Coconut & Ginger: Add ½ cup of chopped glace ginger and ½ of cup chopped walnuts to the wet mix. ½ cup of chopped glace cherries may be added as well if desired.

Coconut & Pineapple: Add 1 cup of crushed tinned pineapple to the wet mix and reduce the milk or yoghurt to 1 cup. Do not use fresh pineapple.

Topping: ¼ cup sugar and ¼ cup dessicated coconut.

Coffee Streusel

Ingredients

Wet Mix
¼ cup butter
½ cup brown sugar
2 eggs
1½ cups plain yoghurt

Dry Mix
3 cups self-raising flour
½ teaspoon cinnamon
½ cup chopped walnuts or pecans
and if desired ½ cup sultanas

Method:

Preheat the oven and grease the pans. Blend the butter and sugar and beat in the eggs and yoghurt. Fold the previously combined dry mix into the wet mix and place in the muffin pans.Blend the topping ingredients together and place this on the top of the muffins pressing it slightly into the muffin batter to help it stick to the muffin top.

Makes 15

Bake: 200⁰C for 20 minutes

Variations

Topping: 1 tablespoon brown sugar, 1 tablespoon margarine, 1 teaspoon cinnamon, 2 tablespoons walnuts.

Comment:

This classic flavour combination of sugar, spice and nuts makes one of the nicest muffins to accompany coffee. It is even more interesting served with honey or walnut butter.

Cheese & Herb

Ingredients

Wet Mix
1 egg, beaten
2 tablespoons margarine or oil
¾ cup grated cheese
½ small onion finely diced
1 teaspoon dried mixed herbs
2 tablespoons chopped parsley
½ cup milk

Dry Mix
2 cups self-raising flour
1 tablespoon sugar, (optional)
1 teaspoon salt
pinch of chilli or cayenne

Method:
Preheat the oven and grease the muffin pans. Place wet mix in a bowl and stir well. Gently stir in the dry mix. Place the mixture into the well greased muffin tins. This mixture is firmer than for most other muffins.

Makes 10-12

Bake: 200⁰ for 25-30 mins.

Variations

Savoury Ham: Add ½ cup of chopped ham to the wet mix ingredients.
Savoury Salmon: Add 1 small jar of smoked salmon cuttings to the wet mix.
Cheese: Omit the herbs from the wet mix, and increase the cheese to 1½ cups.

Suggestions:
Sprinkle a little grated cheese on the top of each muffin before baking. Toasted sesame seeds added to the topping are very nice.

Cheese & Apple Muffins

Cheese & Apple

Ingredients

Wet Mix
2 eggs, beaten
¼ cup honey
¼ cup melted margarine
1 cup sharp cheese, grated
½ cup yoghurt or milk
1 cup finely chopped apple

Dry Mix
2 cups self-raising flour
½ teaspoon baking soda

Method:
Preheat the oven and grease the muffin pans. Combine the wet mix and add the previously combined dry mix. Fold gently together until just mixed. Place in muffin pans and bake.

Makes 12

Bake: 200⁰C for 20 minutes.

Variations

Cheese, Apple & Date: Add ½ cup chopped dates to the wet mix.

Corn Meal

Ingredients

Wet Mix
2 eggs, beaten
½ cup oil
1½ cups plain yoghurt
1½ cups canned creamed corn
¼ cup maple syrup

Dry Mix
1 cup cornmeal
1½ cups self-raising flour
½ teaspoon baking soda

Method:

Preheat the oven and grease the muffin pans. Thoroughly blend all the wet mix ingredients. Combine the dry mix ingredients well before adding them to the wet mix. Stir well. Place in greased muffin pans and bake.

Makes 12

Bake: 200ºC for 20-25 minutes.

Comment:

These muffins have a very pleasant and subtle flavour. When served with maple syrup or honey butter they are a real treat and will certainly join the "repeat performance" ranks. Try these muffins with barbecued chicken and a fresh salad or with creamy pumpkin or tomato soups.

Savoury Cornmeal

Ingredients

Wet Mix   *2 eggs, beaten*
½ cup oil
1 cup sharp cheese, grated
1½ cups canned creamed corn
1 cup plain yoghurt
1 finely diced onion
½ cup diced cooked bacon

Dry Mix   *1½ cups cornmeal*
1½ cups self-raising flour
½ teaspoon baking soda
2 tablespoons sugar

Method:

Preheat the oven and grease the muffin pans. Thoroughly combine the wet mix ingredients. Mix well with the previously combined dry mix. Place in greased muffin pans and bake.

Makes 12-14

Bake: 200°C for 25-30 minutes.

Variations

Parsley Cornmeal: Add ½ cup of chopped parsley to the wet mix.

Date Muffins

Ingredients

Wet Mix
½ cup water
1 cup dates, chopped
2 eggs
½ cup margarine
¼ cup golden syrup, or sugar
½ cup milk

Dry Mix   *2½ cups self-raising flour*
Method:
Preheat the oven and grease the muffin pans. Soak dates in the water for ½ hour. Add the remaining wet mix ingredients and combine. Gently but thoroughly stir in the flour. Place in muffin pans and bake.

Makes 10

Bake: 200⁰C for 20 minutes.

Variation

Date & Orange or Lemon: Omit the milk and replace this with ¾ cup of pureed orange or lemon.
Date & Oatbran: Do not add the egg yolks to the wet mix. Replace the sugar with ½ cup of honey. Replace the 2½ cups of self-raising flour with 1 cup of oatbran, 1 cup of self-raising flour and 1 teaspoon of baking powder.

Fig Muffins

Ingredients

Wet Mix   ½ cup oil
½ cup sugar
2 eggs
½ cup milk
½ orange juice
2 teaspoons orange rind
1 cup chopped dried figs

Dry Mix   2½ cups self-raising flour
¼ teaspoon baking soda

Method:
Preheat the oven and grease the muffin pans. Thoroughly blend all the wet mix ingredients lastly adding the figs, and then gently fold the dry mix into the wet mix. Place the mixture in the prepared pans and bake.

Makes 10-12

Bake: 200°C for 20-25 minutes.

Variations

Fig & Oatbran: See Oatbran Dried Fruit Muffins
Fig & Ginger: Add ½ cup of chopped preserved ginger to the wet mix.

Gingerbread Muffins

Ginger Muffins

Ingredients

Wet Mix
½ cup margarine
¼ cup golden syrup
1 teaspoon molasses
¼ cup sugar
2 eggs
1 cup milk
1 teaspoon grated lemon rind

Dry Mix
2½ cups self-raising flour
¼ teaspoon baking soda
1 teaspoon cinnamon
1 teaspoon mixed spice
1 tablespoon ground ginger

Method:

Preheat the oven and grease the muffin pans. Blend together the margarine, golden syrup, molasses and sugar then beat in the eggs and milk. Combine the dry ingredients then mix them into the wet mix. Place the mixture into the previously greased muffin pans and bake.

Makes 10

Bake: 220⁰C for 20-25 minutes.

Variations

Ginger & Apple: Reduce the milk to ½ cup and add 1 cup diced cooked or 1 cup grated raw apple to the wet mix.

Ginger & Sultana: Add ½ cup sultanas to the wet mix.

Chunky Ginger: Add ¼ cup chopped mixed peel and ¼ cup crystallized ginger to the wet mix.

Raisin & Walnut Ginger: Add ½ cup chopped raisins and ½ cup chopped walnuts to the wet mix.

Ginger & Chocolate: Add 1 cup chopped chocolate or 1 cup chocolate drops to the wet mix. Omit the lemon rind.

Honey Muffins.

Honey Muffins

Ingredients

Wet Mix
½ cup margarine
½ cup honey
2 eggs
½ teaspoon vanilla
1 cup yoghurt

Dry Mix
2 cups self-raising flour
½ teaspoon nutmeg (optional)
1 teaspoon cinnamon (optional)

Method:

Grease the muffin pans and preheat the oven. Blend the margarine and honey. Beat in the eggs then the vanilla and yoghurt. Gently, but thoroughly fold in the dry mix. Place in the greased pans and bake.

Makes 10
Bake: 200°C for 20 minutes.

Variations

Honey & Walnut: Add ½ cup chopped walnuts to the combined wet mix.

Honey & Apple: Add 1 cup diced cooked apple or 1 cup grated raw apple to the combined wet mix. ½ cup walnuts may be added if desired.

Honey & Orange: Reduce the yoghurt to ½ cup. Add ½ cup of pureed whole orange to the combined wet mix.

Honey & Cinnamon: Replace the nutmeg with an extra 2 teaspoons cinnamon.

Honey & Muesli: Increase the yoghurt to 1½ cups. Reduce the self-raising flour to 1½ cups and add 1 cup toasted muesli and ¼ teaspoon baking soda to the dry mix.

Honey & Peanut Butter: Reduce the margarine to ¼ cup and add ½ cup of peanut butter and ¼ cup milk to the wet mix.

Honey & Oatbran: Replace 1 cup self-raising flour with 1 cup of oatbran and 1 teaspoon baking powder. Add 2 teaspoons cinnamon.

Maple Syrup: Replace the honey in the wet mix with maple syrup and add ½ cup of chopped walnuts or pecans and 1 teaspoon vanilla essence. Omit the nutmeg.

Malty Muffins

Ingredients

Wet Mix
½ cup margarine
½ cup sugar
½ cup powdered malt
2 eggs
1½ cups milk
1 teaspoon vanilla essence

Dry Mix
1½ cups self-raising flour
1 cup wholemeal self-raising flour

Method:

Preheat the oven and grease the muffin pans. Blend the margarine, sugar and malt. Beat in the eggs, milk and vanilla. Combine the dry mix flours and add this to the wet mix. Gently stir the mixture until all ingredients are blended. Place in the prepared pans and bake.

Note: If the mixture is too stiff, don't be afraid to add a little extra milk or water so that the mixing spoon moves easily through the batter. The mixture should not be so runny that it cannot be scooped in one movement into the muffin pan.

Makes 12

Bake: 200ºC for 20 minutes.

Variations

Malt and Raisin: Add one cup of chopped raisins to the wet mix.
Malt & Walnut: Add one cup of chopped walnuts to the wet mix.

Oatbran Muffins —

Oatbran

Ingredients

Wet Mix   ½ cup oil
½ cup sugar
2 egg whites
1 cup skim milk

Dry Mix   1½ cups self-raising flour
1 cup oatbran
1 teaspoon baking powder

Method:
Preheat the oven and grease the muffin pans. Thoroughly blend the wet mix ingredients. Stir the previously combined dry mix into the wet mix. Unlike other muffin mixtures, this mixture should be quite creamy in consistency. The mixture would need to be ladled into the muffin pans rather than spooned into them.

Makes 10

Bake: 180⁰C for 20 minutes.

Variations

Oatbran & Dried Fruit: Reduce the milk to ½ cup and add ½ cup of orange or lemon puree (the whole fruit pureed in whiz or blender) to the wet mixture. Add ½ to 1 cup desired dried fruits such as sultanas, currants, figs, apricots etc. to the wet mix.

Oatbran & Blueberry: Reduce the milk to ½ cup. Add ½ cup lemon puree and 1 tin drained blueberries to the wet mix. Take care not to break the blueberries when mixing.

Comment:
These muffins make really valuable addition to a low cholesterol diet. All Muffins can be easily made cholesterol free by omitting the egg yolks; using vegetable oil and skim milk.

Sesame Seeds

Peanut Butter

Ingredients

Wet Mix
¼ cup sugar
¼ cup butter or margarine
½ cup peanut butter
2 eggs
1½ cups milk

Dry Mix
2½ cups self-raising flour
¼ teaspoon baking soda

Method:

Preheat the oven and grease the muffin pans. Blend thoroughly the sugar, margarine and peanut butter. Beat in the eggs and milk. Fold the dry mix into the wet mix. Place the mixture in the prepared pans. Sprinkle with cinnamon sugar and bake.

Makes 10-15

Bake: 200⁰C for 15-20 minutes

Variations

Peanut Butter & Chocolate Chip: Add ½ cup of chopped chocolate or ½ cup of chocolate chips and ½ teaspoon vanilla to the wet mix.

Peanut Butter & Date or Raisin: Add ½ cup of chopped dates or raisins to the combined wet mix.

Peanut Butter & Sesame Seed: Add ½ cup toasted sesame seeds to the combined wet mix. Add ½ cup chopped dates if desired.

Topping: Cinnamon Sugar—See Avocado Muffins

Poppy Seed & Lemon Muffins

Poppy Seed & Lemon

Ingredients

Wet Mix
½ cup margarine
½ cup sugar
2 eggs
1 cup milk or yoghurt
2 teaspoons grated lemon rind
½ cup lemon juice
¼ cup poppy seeds

Dry Mix
2 cups self-raising flour
¼ teaspoon baking soda

Method:
Preheat the oven and grease the muffin pans. Blend the margarine and sugar and beat in the eggs, milk, lemon and poppy seeds. Fold the dry mix into the wet mix, spoon into the muffin pans and bake.

Makes 12

Bake: 200°C for 20 minutes.

Comment:
These muffins are delicious served with lemon butter or honey butter. Using yoghurt in the wet mix gives a moister product.

Potato Muffins

Ingredients

Wet Mix   *1 cup mashed potato*
1½ cups milk
2 eggs
½ cup yoghurt or sour cream
½ cup finely chopped spring onions

Dry Mix   *2½ cups self-raising flour*
1 teaspoon salt

Method:

Preheat the oven and thoroughly grease the muffin pans. Blend the potato, milk, egg and yoghurt or cream. Stir in the chopped onions. Fold the flour and salt into the wet mix. Place in the prepared pans and bake.

Makes 12

Bake: 200ºC for 20-25 minutes.

Variations

Potato & Ham: Add ½ cup finely chopped ham to the wet mix.

Potato & Parsley: Add 2 tablespoons chopped fresh parsley to the wet mix.

Potato, Ham & Apple: Omit the onion and add 1 cup peeled and diced apple.

Pumpkin

Ingredients

Wet Mix *¼ cup margarine*
½ cup sugar
2 eggs
1 cup pumpkin puree*
* Puree is made from 300g of pumpkin cooked in ¼ cup liquid.

Dry Mix *2½ cups self-raising flour*

Method:
Preheat the oven and prepare the muffin pans. Thoroughly blend the margarine and sugar then beat in the eggs and pumpkin puree. Fold the flour in the wet mix and place in the prepared pans. Sprinkle with cinnamon sugar and bake.

Makes 10 - 12

Bake: 200⁰C for 20 - 25 minutes.

Variations

Pumpkin & Orange: Puree 1 whole orange (this includes the skin) and add this to the wet mix. Increase the self-raising flour to 3 cups.

Spiced Pumpkin: Reduce the sugar to ¼ cup and add ¼ cup of treacle to the wet mix. ½ cup chopped raisins and walnuts may be added if desired. Add ½ teaspoon ground cinnamon, ½ teaspoon ground nutmeg, ½ teaspoon ground ginger and ¼ teaspoon baking soda to the dry mix.

Sweet Potato: Substitute the pumpkin puree with sweet potato puree. Extra milk may be required to mix to a moist enough consistency.

Pumpkin & Prune: Add ½ cup chopped prunes to the Pumpkin & Orange wet mix.

Topping: Cinnamon Sugar (Equal parts of sugar and cinnamon mixed together).

Refrigerator Muffins.

Refrigerator

Ingredients

Wet Mix   2 cups boiling water
2 cups rolled oats
1 cup oil
2 cups brown sugar
4 eggs
1 kilo plain low fat yoghurt or buttermilk
2 cups mixed dried fruits

Dry Mix   3 cups wholemeal flour
2 cups plain flour
4 cups allbran or flaky bran
4 teaspoons baking soda.

Method:
Combine the rolled oats and boiling water in a bowl and allow to cool. Thoroughly combine the oil, sugar, eggs and yoghurt and stir in the mixed fruits. Add to the soaked oats.

Combine the dry mix and then thoroughly mix into the wet mix. **Keep this batter in a sealed container in the refrigerator for up to 6 weeks. Gently mix before placing into prepared pans to bake.**

Makes 40 - 50 muffins

Bake: 200⁰C for 20 - 25 minutes for 12 muffins.

Microwave: 6 muffins in microwave pans for 5 minutes on high.

Comment:
These muffins are a boost for the frantic mother or wife. If necessary your family can cook their own muffins! They are such fun to watch cooking.

Rhubarb

Ingredients

Wet Mix *2 eggs*
¼ cup oil
¾ cup sugar
2 cups milk
½ cup yoghurt or sour cream
1 teaspoon vanilla
2 cups finely chopped fresh rhubarb

Dry Mix *4 cups self-raising flour*
½ teaspoon baking soda
½ teaspoon cinnamon

Method:
Preheat the oven and grease the muffin pans. Thoroughly blend all the wet mix ingredients lastly adding the rhubarb. Fold in the previously combined dry mix. Place in muffin pans, sprinkle with cinnamon sugar and bake.

Makes 18

Bake: 200⁰C for 25 minutes.

Topping: Cinnamon Sugar (see Pumpkin Muffins)

Smarty Party

Ingredients

Wet Mix   ½ cup margarine
½ cup sugar
2 eggs
1 cup milk
1 cup smarties

Dry Mix   2½ cups self-raising flour

Method:

Preheat the oven and grease the muffin pans. Use paper cases for these muffins. It is best to use cup cake size pans for these muffins. Thoroughly blend the margarine and sugar and beat in the eggs and milk. Quickly mix in the smarties and then gently fold in the flour. Place in paper cases lining the pans. Put an extra smartie or two on top of each muffin before baking, to make them look more colourful.

Makes 36

Bake: 200⁰C for 20 minutes.

Comment:
Suprisingly, the cooked smarties inside these little muffins become soft and creamy. They really make a party treat and will leave chocolate crackles for 'snap crackle & pop'.

Strawberry Muffins

Strawberry

Ingredients

Wet Mix   *¼ cup butter*
¼ cup sugar
2 eggs
½ cup milk
1 cup strawberry yoghurt

Dry Mix   *2 cups self-raising flour*
¼ teaspoon baking soda

Method:

Preheat the oven and grease the muffin pans.
Blend together the butter and sugar then beat
in the eggs, milk and yoghurt. Gently combine
the dry mix with the wet mix. Place the
mixture into the previously prepared pans.
Paper liners are suitable for these muffins.

Place ½ teaspoon strawberry jam on the top of each
muffin. Slightly press the jam into the raw mixture
to avoid it running away during baking. Bake the
muffins.

Makes 10-12 muffins

Bake: 200⁰C for 20 minutes.

Topping: Strawberry jam.

Comment:

Any flavour of yoghurt or jam topping may be used,
e.g. cherry yoghurt with plum jam topping.
These muffins are popular with children and great
for lunch boxes. It is not necessary to butter
them.

Pritikin Muffins

Ingredients

Wet Mix:
4 egg whites
¾ cup skim milk
½ cup non fat yoghurt
¼ cup apple juice concentrate
2 apples, peeled and chopped
Grated rind of 1 lemon
1 cup drained morello cherries
½ cup sultanas

Dry Mix:
1½ cups wholemeal flour
1 cup rolled oats
1 cup oatbran
3 teaspoons baking powder
1½ teaspoons cinnamon

Method:

Preheat the oven and prepare the muffin pans.

Thoroughly beat together the egg whites, skim milk, yoghurt and apple juice, then mix in the apples, lemon rind, cherries and sultanas.

Combine the dry mix and then fold into the wet mix. Spoon into the prepared muffin pans and bake.

Makes 12

Bake 180⁰ 25-30 minutes.

FLAVOURED BUTTERS
FOR MUFFINS

Honey Butter: Add ¼ cup honey to 1 cup butter or margarine and beat until light and fluffy. Recommended with pumpkin, bran, apple, corn, orange, banana and ginger muffins.

Orange Butter: Add ¼ cup orange juice, grated rind of 2 oranges and ¼ cup of icing sugar to 1 cup butter or margarine. Beat until light and fluffy.

Cream Cheese Butter: Beat together equal parts of cream cheese and butter with added flavours such as honey or liqueurs. This spread is particularly delicious.

Hazelnut Butter: Add ¼ cup finely chopped hazelnuts and ¼ cup icing sugar to 1 cup of butter, margarine or cream cheese. Blend thoroughly.
A dash of rum makes it a very daring spread.
This is delicious with ginger or avocado muffins.

Almond Butter: Make as for hazelnut butter.

THE INSIDE STORY OF MUFFINS

MUFFINS HAVE SEVEN PARTS
WHAT DOES EACH PART DO?

1. EGGS—Whole eggs, egg whites

Eggs help the muffins to rise—especially the whites. The yolks help to blend the ingredients more easily by their emulsifying action. Eggs moisten and tenderise as well.

2. SWEETENERS—White, brown, raw, or caster sugars, golden syrup, treacle, molasses or honey. Flavoured syrups, e.g. maple syrup, jams and preserves, Artificial sweeteners.

Sugar or its substitute i.e. honey or flavoured syrups or both provide sweetness and flavour but also tenderise the muffins.

3. SHORTENERS—Margarine, oil, cream, sour cream, cream cheese, butter.

Shorteners make muffins more moist and rich. They aid in keeping the mixture tender and help prevent overmixing.

4. LIQUIDS—Milk (skim, buttermilk, etc.) yoghurt, cream, fruit juice, fruit and vegetable purees, flavoured syrups.

Liquids help combine the ingredients but can also provide flavour to the mixture. Fruit juice and purees and yoghurts are most commonly used as well as syrups.

5. FLOURS—White and wholemeal flours, etc., selfraising flours, flaked bran or allbran, rolled oats or oatbran, polenta, rice flour etc.

Most muffins need some flour. Using all oatbran or polenta gives a very heavy and crumbly muffin. Combinations of "flours" gives very good results. Flour forms the bones of the muffin.

6. FLAVOURS—Fruit-dried, fresh or canned, nuts, herbs, spices, chocolate, syrups, vegetables-fresh or canned.

Freshly diced or grated fruits or vegetables make moist and tasty muffins. Flavoured butters make interesting additions. Peanut butter is the most common addition. Previously blended flavour additions usually become easily masked e.g., it is better to add dried apricots rather than apricot jam to achieve an apricot flavour.

Anything which is desirable and paletable can provide flavour in a muffin. Most commonly used are dried fruits and nuts, spices, syrups, chopped chocolate and cocoa. Savoury flavours are very acceptable and cheeses with onion and ham or drained tinned corn are an example.

7. RAISING AGENTS—Self-raising flour, baking powder, baking soda, yeast.

Self-raising flour produces good results with muffins. This is flour mixed with baking powder. An addition of baking soda will often produce a lighter fluffier muffin. Baking soda must be used with an acid to activate it e.g. cream of tartar, golden syrup, molasses or fruit acids. Your recipe will guide you.

If you want to experiment with muffins and their magic, the following recipe will provide a good base to work from. To begin with, don't stray too far from home and soon you will find that you are confident enough with the results to have some really good fun. The liberties you can take are quite wide and muffins are friendly and helpful. You will soon have learnt the magic.

BASIC MUFFIN RECIPE

Ingredients

Wet Mix   *¼ cup butter*
½ cup sugar
2 eggs
1 cup milk

Dry Mix   *2½ cups self-raising flour*

Method:
Prepare the muffin pans by greasing them well or lining with papers. Preheat the oven. Blend thoroughly the butter and sugar. Beat in the eggs and then the milk. Carefully mix in the flour taking care not to overmix. Place the mixture in the prepared pans and bake.

Makes 10-12

Bake: 200ºC for 20-25 minutes.

YOUR NOTES.